THE HOLOCAUST

Aftermath of the Holocaust

Jane Shuter

Heinemann Library
Chicago, Illinois

Designed by Joanna Sapwell and Tinstar Design
Illustrations by Martin Griffin
Originated by Ambassador Litho Ltd
Printed in China, by Wing King Tong

07 06 05 04 03
10 9 8 7 6 5 4 3 2 1

Library of Congress
Cataloging-in-Publication Data
Shuter, Jane.
  Aftermath of the Holocaust / Jane Shuter.
    p. cm. -- (The Holocaust)
    Includes bibliographical references and index.
Contents: Last days of Nazi rule -- Liberation -- The liberated – The defeated -- Ordinary people -- Rebuilding Europe -- What about Germany? -- Rebuilding lives -- Justice -- On trial at Nuremburg -- Eichmann -- A closer look: Caught in the aftermath.
  ISBN 1-4034-0807-6 (HC) 1-4034-3199-X (Pbk.)
  1. Holocaust, Jewish (1939-1945)--Juvenile literature.
2. Holocaust survivors--Biography--Juvenile literature.
[1. Holocaust, Jewish (1939-1945) 2. Holocaust survivors. 3. Jews--History--1945- 4. Jews--Europe.] I. Title. II. Holocaust
(Chicago, Ill.)
  D804.34 .S63 2002
  940.53'18--dc21
                2002006752

Acknowledgments
The author and publisher are grateful to the following for permission to reproduce copyright material: pp. 4, 8 AKG; pp. 5, 14 Robert Hunt Picture Library; p. 6 Mary Evans Picture Library; pp. 9, 28, 33, 36, 38, 40, 41, 45, 47 USHMM; p. 10 Hulton Getty; pp. 11, 13, 17 Lee Miller Archive; p. 12 Popperfoto; pp. 15, 21, 22, 25, 26 Hulton Archive; p. 18 Tomi Ungerer & Diogenes Verlag/AG Zurich; pp. 24, 44 Wieslaw M. Zielínski/ Aushwitz-Birkenau State Museum; p. 29 Martin Gilbert; p. 30 Yad Vashem; p. 31 Jerry Cooke/Corbis; p. 32 Unknown; p. 34 Ullstein Bild; p. 35 Robert Harding Picture Library; p. 37 Rich Cohen; pp. 39, 43 Topham Picturepoint; p. 42 Bridgeman Art Library; pp. 46, 48, 49 Kitty Hart-Moxon/House of Stratus

Cover photograph reproduced with the permission of USHMM.

Special thanks to Ronald Smelser and Sally Brown-Winter.

About the series consultants
Ronald Smelser is a history professor at the University of Utah. He has written or edited eight books on the Holocaust and Nazi Germany and over three dozen articles. His recent publications include *Learning About the Holocaust: A Student Guide* (4 vol.) and *Lessons and Legacies: The Holocaust and Justice*. Professor Smelser is also a past president of the German Studies Association.

Sally Brown-Winter has worked in the field of Jewish Education as a principal and teacher for over 25 years. In her schools, the Shoah—its history, lessons, and implications—have been explored from kindergarten through high school.

Every effort has been made to contact copyright holders of any material reproduced in this book. Any omissions will be rectified in subsequent printings if notice is given to the publisher.

Some words are shown in bold, **like this.** You can find out what they mean by looking in the glossary.

Contents

The Holocaust

In 1933 the **Nazi** Party, led by Adolf Hitler, came to power in Germany. It wanted to create a new German empire, the **Third Reich,** with Hitler as its leader, or *Führer*.

The Camp System

The Nazis wanted total obedience from the German people. As soon as they came to power, the Nazis began arresting anyone they saw as a political opponent. They set up special prison **camps** for these people. The camps, known as **concentration camps,** were different from ordinary prisons because all of the prisoners were imprisoned without trial and had no release date. They lived in appalling conditions and they died, or were killed, in large numbers. Soon the Nazis began filling the camps with people they saw as **undesirable,** either because of their nationality, their religious beliefs, or their behavior. The people Hitler saw as most undesirable were **Jewish** people.

Anti-Semitism

Once the Nazis were in power, it became official government policy to be **anti-Semitic** and act against Jews by passing laws that stripped them of their rights, by throwing them out of the country, and by acting violently against them.

Invasion

The Nazis began to take over other countries in Europe to enlarge their empire. Between 1938 and 1941, Germany sent its army marching both east and west across Europe. People in the countries they took over were forced to obey Nazi laws. In all Nazi-controlled lands, including Germany, even in the German army itself, there were people who supported the Nazis and others who did not.

Nazi Propaganda

The Nazis often twisted the truth to make people believe their views. When they took over Poland in 1939, they published a series of articles in Germany called "The *Führer's* Soldiers in the Field." This photo, published in the articles, was labeled: "Polish Jews doing unaccustomed work," implying that Polish Jews never worked hard.

4

The Holocaust

The Nazis believed that they had to make their new empire *Judenfrei*—Jew-free. At first, they simply tried to force Jews out of the lands they controlled. Once they were at war, they began shutting Jewish people up in **ghettos,** parts of cities where only Jews were allowed to live. Then, they sent Jews to the camps and, finally, they set up **death camps.** The sole purpose of the death camps was to kill Jewish people, usually by gassing thousands of victims every day.

This mass murder is now often referred to as the **Holocaust.** Jews were not the only victims. Other peoples, such as Gypsies and Poles, were also seen by the Nazis as separate, "inferior," **races.** Other victims were those who did not fit the Nazi ideas about a perfect state, including the physically and mentally disabled, homosexuals, and political opponents of the Nazis.

How Do We Know?

We know about the effects of the Holocaust from many different sources. One of the most important is the evidence of survivors. They have left written and spoken evidence, as well as photos and paintings. Their relatives, especially their children and friends, can also pass on this evidence.

When the camps were liberated, the **Allied** soldiers and aid workers also recorded what they saw, as did the reporters who followed them. These people and the survivors have been interviewed since the end of the war, on radio, on TV, and for museum records.

The **SS** and other Nazis have been less willing to speak about the Holocaust and its effects. However, those who were caught were brought to trial for war crimes and the evidence used in these trials tells us about the Holocaust. While much of the camps and the documentary evidence was destroyed by the SS, some survived.

Liberated in Auschwitz

As the Soviet army moved into German-occupied Poland, they found and liberated the many camps that the SS had left behind. This photo was taken as the Soviet armies liberated Auschwitz camp.

The Third Reich Crumbles

By June 1941, the German army had to defend borders in the west, south, and east of Europe. The army also had to keep its **occupied** countries under control. The **Allies** began to move into the **Reich** from all sides. In 1943–44 British and American troops attacked the Mediterranean and the French coast. In the east, Hitler had expected the German army to have beaten the Russians before the winter of 1941–42. However, Russian troops pushed the German army steadily back toward Germany all through 1943, and in 1944, they began to **liberate** other countries that bordered Russia, such as Poland. As they advanced, the Soviet troops found camps and began to uncover the extent of the **Holocaust.** Soon British and American troops began liberating camps, too.

An End to the Holocaust?

As the Allies reached Berlin on April 30, 1945, Hitler shot himself. On May 2 the Germany armies in Italy surrendered. On May 5 the German armies in Denmark, the Netherlands, and north Germany surrendered. On May 7 what was left of the German government surrendered entirely. The end of the war stopped the mass killing. However, the effects of the Holocaust did not end when the war ended and the Nazis lost control of Europe. The Holocaust still affects those who survived, their children and other family members. It also affects many people who were not victims, including Nazis, members of the **SS,** and their families.

Millions Murdered

The Holocaust resulted in the deaths of huge numbers of people. Historians have tried hard to figure out how many people were killed in the Holocaust.

The Defeat of Germany

This map shows how the Allies closed in on Germany from all sides from 1943.

→ British and American forces
→ Soviet forces
➡ Allied bombing raids on Germany from 1940

0   500 km
0   500 miles

Their work suggests that between 5.1 and 5.8 million people were murdered. In many cases, only one or two members of a family survived. In addition to their **Jewish** victims, the Nazis also murdered over 200,000 European Gypsies and hundreds of thousands of Russians, Poles, and members of **resistance** movements.

Who Knew?

One question about the Holocaust that is still argued about today is who knew about the Holocaust and supported Nazi policies against the Jews. Some historians argue that only a few people knew and that only a few people supported the Nazis' killing of the Jews. Other people argue that the Holocaust would have been impossible to carry out without the support of many "ordinary" Germans. In Germany, in the army, and in occupied countries, there were probably many different levels of knowledge and support. Norbert Lebert was

just fifteen when the war ended. He had been an enthusiastic member of the **Hitler Youth** and played with the children of Nazi leaders. He remembers the reaction of many people after the war:

These people said "I know my father, my brother, my friend, my husband. They would never do such a thing. They knew nothing, they can't have known anything. And if they did know something, they must have been led astray by the real devils, the few who really knew."

Yet Norbert felt that he was saved in some way by the end of the war. He had been swept along by events and would have become part of the system, done whatever the party demanded: "Given my unconditional enthusiasm at the time, there's no reason to think things would have turned out any other way."

Last Days of Nazi Rule

The last few months of **Nazi** rule in Europe were chaotic. The **Allies** were advancing from a number of different directions. Many German soldiers were killed or captured. Some fled the army and the fighting and tried to make their way home to their families. Soldiers who stayed loyal to the Nazis often had to deal with several sets of orders from Berlin that contradicted each other. For example, **Jewish** prisoners were still being **transported** to Auschwitz from France and the Netherlands. Meanwhile, other prisoners were being marched out of Auschwitz for fear of the advancing Russian troops. The Nazi administration, always more organized on paper than in real life, fell apart.

Destroying the Evidence

As the German army retreated westward beginning in the autumn of 1944, the **SS** were ordered to close down the **concentration camps** and destroy as much evidence as possible. It was especially important to destroy the **death camps.** With the Allies advancing quickly, though, many camp commanders panicked and simply marched all of the inmates back toward Germany. Before leaving, the SS destroyed what papers they could and killed all of the sick and weak prisoners they could find.

Many camp commanders rushed their escape and some prisoners hid from the guards who were ordered to do the killing. In Buchenwald camp, Israel Lau's brother, Naftali, saved him by hiding him in a pile of corpses. Naftali told Israel to lie still while the SS cleared the camp. He was still lying there when the American army **liberated** the camp the next day. He was eight years old.

Obvious Effects

One of the most obvious effects of the **Holocaust** on survivors was that almost all of them were sick, starved, and homeless. These survivors were photographed in Buchenwald camp soon after it was liberated.

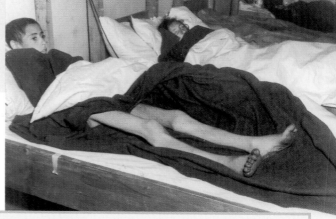

Death Marches

The death marches took place from January 1945 onward, in awful winter weather. The words "death march" suggest that people walked steadily from one place to another. The death marches were not like that. People did not always walk, and those walking were seldom well enough to do so. Some were piled into coal trucks or cattle cars and taken by train. Prisoners who fell behind, tried to escape, or did anything to annoy the SS in charge were killed. Sometimes they could no longer keep walking and were left to die in the snow. Sometimes, the SS decided it just was not worth marching their prisoners any further, so they killed them all and then deserted. Trains sometimes spent days stopped on the tracks. At least one

A Survivor

This photograph shows two of the 620 survivors from the five-week death march of 1,200 prisoners from Grunberg to Helmbrechts. This march had a high survival rate because half of the prisoners were not Jewish. The SS had orders to treat non-Jewish prisoners more carefully than the Jewish ones who the SS saw as less than human because of Nazi ideas about **race.**

train was left stopped until all but a handful of the prisoners in the locked trucks were dead. On average, only a third of the prisoners in a death march survived.

Different Orders

Even if the SS marched their prisoners to another camp, the prisoners' troubles were not over. Roman Frister, a Polish Jew, remembers his march from a **labor camp** near Vienna to Mauthausen. He set off with 1,027 other prisoners. Only 322 prisoners, including Roman, reached Mauthausen:

The SS major in charge of the camp came towards us, arms outstretched.

"I'm sorry. This camp is not accepting any more prisoners."

"I have a written order," our SS officer said.

"I can't help. This camp is overflowing. My orders are to take no more. I will not take your 300 corpses because we have no room for them, no food for them, and no one to guard them. We don't even have any gas left to gas them. You've got machine guns. Finish them off yourself."

At that point a third officer arrived. He said half of us could come in, half stay outside, no matter what. I made sure I got in. I never found out what happened to those left outside.

Liberation

Soldiers of the **Allied** armies—American, Russian, and British—**liberated** different camps. We now know there were different kinds of camps: **death camps, concentration camps,** and **labor camps.** At the end of the war, the differences were less clear. The death marches had piled prisoners from all of the camps into camps in or near Germany. Certainly, the liberating soldiers could not see any difference in the camps. In all of them there were dying people, infectious diseases, and huge piles of starved bodies.

Telling the World

Almost all of the soldiers, nurses, and aid workers who went into the camps say that what they found was "indescribable." One young soldier from the United States said:

> *You couldn't describe it. You had to use words like "terrible," "inhuman," and*

"evil"—all used before for less bad things. You couldn't talk about how you felt because you had to use words like "helpless" and "angry." You needed a whole other set of words for it.

The British reporter Richard Dimbleby went to Belsen camp in Germany in April 1945, shortly after it was liberated by British soldiers. He sent a report back to Britain stressing over and over that he was not exaggerating:

> *I picked my way over corpse after corpse in the gloom. I came across a girl, impossible to tell her age, her yellow skin tight across her face, with two dark holes for eyes. She stretched out her stick of an arm and gasped, "English, English, medicine, medicine." Beyond her, down the passage and into the hut, dying people shifted, unable to raise themselves from the floor.*

Dachau

The American soldiers who liberated Dachau, like all of the liberators, had to collect and bury hundreds of dead people. They recorded it so the deaths could not be denied later.

Killing with Kindness

The soldiers who first arrived at the camps often handed over all of the food they had with them to the starving prisoners. It was a natural reaction. Unfortunately, this food was far richer than prisoners were used to. At best, the prisoners ate the food quickly and had bad stomach upsets. At worst, the strain on their stomachs killed them. The British army that liberated Belsen sent out "Notes on Taking Over a Concentration Camp," warning others of the problems they would face and the mistakes to avoid.

Switching Off

One of the hardest things for the liberators to cope with was the fact that the people they had saved still died. The camps were full of people who were too sick or too weak to be saved. Lieutenant Mervin Gonin, a British doctor sent to Belsen, remembers the disease typhus was raging:

> Five hundred people were dying each day. Five hundred would die every day for weeks, until anything we were doing began to have the slightest effect.

An Accident?

Many soldiers must have realized how hard it would be to find evidence against all of the camp guards and officers and bring them to trial. They did not try to stop prisoners from attacking the guards. This photograph of Dachau shows American soldiers fishing a guard out of the moat that surrounded the camp, where he had "accidentally" drowned.

That doesn't mean it was easy to watch, just because you knew it couldn't be stopped.

Another thing the liberators found difficult was that they had to think in the same way that the **SS** had. They had to see people as a mass. They had to get used to people dying, to stop, as one doctor put it: "imagining them as your aunt, or your mother; your brother, or your father."

They had to be tough and not get emotionally involved in any one case. Thus, they ended up saying to people who asked how they coped with the misery all around them: "You get used to it."

The Liberated

Many **Holocaust** survivors barely remember being **liberated.** They were too ill. Perec Zylberberg was a young man who had been in the Lodz **ghetto** and several slave **labor camps.** He became ill on a death-march train from Buchenwald camp to Terezín, in Czechoslovakia. He says:

*I don't remember arriving. I just wasn't in the wagon anymore. I was in a building, with bunks. I didn't know if the camp was being run by the **Allies** or the Germans. We were registered and I was given a piece of bread. I was told I had to go to the hospital but could take the bread with me. I remember getting violent over that bread. They had to keep showing it to me to calm me down. I didn't want anyone to take it.*

An Amazing Meeting

Most people were liberated by strangers, but Fania Fénelon, a French musician, remembers an amazing meeting when Auschwitz was liberated:

We had been liberated by the infantry, now the motorized units were arriving. Through the window I saw the first jeep enter the camp. An officer jumped out, a Dutchman. He looked around, dazed, then began to run like a madman, arms outstretched, calling, "Margrett, Margrett!" A woman staggered toward him, her striped tatters floating like rags tied to a pole. It was his wife, three-quarters dead, in a frightening state of filth and decay, a smiling ghost. He hugged her to him.

Temporary Relief

The Allied armies liberated many camps when they were still advancing and fighting the Germans. The soldiers could not stay long to help those they liberated. They were followed by relief agencies, such as the Red Cross, who had their hands full looking after the sick. Wherever possible, the army or relief agencies closed the camp and set up a new **Displaced Persons** (**DP**) **camp** for the liberated. Often it was near the old camp—too many people were too sick to be moved far. Those ex-prisoners who could look after themselves were left, like the women in the picture, to scavenge from **SS** stores and equipment dumped by the **Nazis.**

Revenge or Justice?

Many soldiers who arrived in the camps were so horrified by the conditions that they let the prisoners turn on their guards and even encouraged this violence. Perhaps they realized that in the chaos as the Allies advanced, it would be all too easy for the guilty to slip away. The Russians who liberated Terezín told the liberated prisoners that they had 24 hours to do what they wanted to the Germans. There were some killings, but not as many as might have been expected. Chaskiel Rosemblum, a young Jewish boy who had been in a labor camp, remembers:

> We enjoyed bringing a different Nazi into the barracks each day and making him clean it. We made them work hard. But we couldn't kill them. I don't feel especially proud of having been unable to kill the people who assassinated my baby sisters, my brother, my sister, my parents—all six million **Jews.** But I just couldn't. Others could. One ten-year-old who had seen his parents killed was killing one Nazi after the other.

Free or Not?

Some prisoners left their camps at once. Managing for themselves was very hard, especially in a Europe torn apart by war and shortages. Bronka Klibanski, a Polish political prisoner, was liberated in January 1945:

> We were all drunk with happiness. But what then? How to go on? There were no homes left, no families. I went home and wandered through the streets, tears steaming down my cheeks, looking for familiar faces.

The Defeated

Some members of the **SS** ran away as soon as they realized that Germany was defeated. They threw away the uniform they had been so proud of and tried to get as far away from their **camps** as they could. Others left too late. They were captured in the camps, or nearby. Some even waited and officially surrendered to the **Allies.** Perhaps they thought they had more chance of surviving this way—they would have to be treated properly, as prisoners-of-war.

Following Orders

Captured SS guards tried to find excuses for what they had done. They admitted to knowing as little as possible. Where they had to admit that they knew about some dreadful action, or had even done it, they tried to excuse what they had done. One statement was so common it became almost a catch phrase: "I couldn't do anything else. I was only following orders."

Kurt Mobius, an SS officer who worked in Chelmno **death camp,** went even further at his trial and blamed brainwashing by the **Nazi** Party: "It never even entered my head that the orders I was following could be wrong. I believed the **propaganda** that **Jews** were criminals and sub-human."

There is no record of soldiers being shot, or even imprisoned, for refusing to work in a camp, nor for refusing to join one of the *Einsatzgruppen* killing squads in Eastern Europe. Several witnesses in later trials said they had either refused to join a killing squad or refused to gas people and had not been punished as a result. However, the punishment would probably have been execution for the "treason" of disobedience. So, anyone who was punished would not have been alive to say so. The soldiers in the killing squads were supposed to be volunteers. Some were not ashamed, even after the war. One of the *Einsatzgruppen*, Petras Zelionka, said in an interview from prison: "You just pressed the trigger and shot. Some people are just doomed, and that is that. They were all just Jews."

SS Women

These are women guards from Belsen camp, photographed after liberation. They probably all went to trial. The woman at the front on the left, Irma Grese, was tried and hanged in December 1945.

All Bad?

Immediately after the **liberation** of the camps, many Allied soldiers did not distinguish between ordinary German soldiers and the SS who had run the camps. They thought all German soldiers had known about the camps and thus were all responsible for them. Many ordinary soldiers, like this officer in the ruins of Saarbrucken, had to face losing the war and being seen as monsters. German soldiers who fought in western Europe were much less likely to have known about the Holocaust than other soldiers, even those who were not SS or Nazis, who fought Soviet soldiers in the east. Adolf Buchner, who was in an SS unit fighting in the east, is certain that anyone who fought there must have been caught up in mass murder: "There were no scruples, everybody was a target." Soldiers who fought in western Europe were not expected to behave in this way— most of the time.

Escape

Many Nazis escaped after the war. How did they get away? In the chaos after the war, some simply took off their uniforms and pretended to be civilian refugees. This was easiest for guards, *kapos,* and others who were not well known. There were networks called **ratlines** set up before the end of the war to help them escape. The ratlines smuggled Nazis out of Germany. Some settled in Europe, but many went farther away. South America was a popular destination.

Some people who had helped in the **Holocaust** hardly moved at all yet still got away unpunished. Many doctors, nurses, and scientists found it easy to pick up their old professions and go back into civilian life as if they had never left it. Their skills were needed, so the Allies ignored the fact that they might have been guilty of helping the Nazis carry out the Holocaust. The Allies did not investigate the war records of most of these people too closely; they just used their skills.

Ordinary People

Ordinary people in Hitler's Europe reacted to **liberation** in many different ways, just as they had reacted differently to the rise of the **Nazis** in the 1930s. Some people were simply delighted. This was especially true in lands that Germany had taken over—but it was true of some Germans, too. Elsa Gretz, a German woman who lived in Berlin all through the war, remembers:

It was such a relief. We'd had to pretend for so long, turn a blind eye, seem to support the Nazis. Sometimes you look at everyone around you and think they were all doing the same and that if only one person was brave enough to say so you'd all turn around and throw them out. At other times you thought you were the only one against the Nazis and everyone else was watching you. And we'd been at war for so long, too.

Free Again

Most people in countries that had been **occupied** by the Nazis were delighted to be liberated. However, people who had sided with the Nazis and helped them—called collaborators—were far from happy when the Nazis were driven out. In the first months after the war, there was a lot of action against collaborators. They were imprisoned, thrown out of their homes, or executed. Unfortunately some innocent people were punished in the need for revenge, while some of the most active collaborators escaped with Nazi help.

Edith Hahn

Edith Hahn was a **Jewish** woman who had lived out the war in hiding, pretending to be a Christian. She had married an engineer, a member of the Nazi Party who was not fully committed to Nazi ideas. He was called up to fight in 1945. Edith first learned of the **death camps** when she was listening, illegally, to the American radio broadcast, "Voice of America." She remembers her reaction to its description of what was left at Majdanek death camp. As the broadcaster described the gas chambers, the crematoria, the piles of bodies, bones, and human ashes, Edith thought of her family.

He went on to describe the piles of clothes and shoes, including those belonging to small children. Edith remembers her reaction:

*No, I thought, this is impossible. This is someone's **propaganda.** It can't be. No. I wanted to move, to turn it off, to make him [the broadcaster] stop. But I couldn't move. And he didn't stop.*

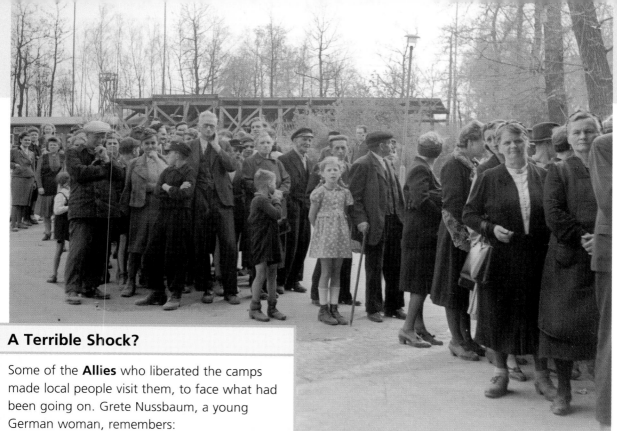

A Terrible Shock?

Some of the **Allies** who liberated the camps made local people visit them, to face what had been going on. Grete Nussbaum, a young German woman, remembers:

> Mother and I—I was just sixteen—were among those forced by the Americans to tour Dachau. I'll never forget those heaps of starved corpses. . . . Mother had a nervous breakdown.

Full of Kindness

Many camp survivors remember people feeding them, giving them a place to stay, doing everything they could to help after the war. Many survivors especially praise the people of Czechoslovakia for their kindness. Moniek Goldberg remembered:

> When we arrived in Prague we went to a hotel. They wouldn't hear of us paying. We sold some cigarettes to get some Czech money to pay our way around. But wherever we went, to a restaurant, to a cinema or a concert, they refused our money. All they said was: "Z Koncentraku" (from a concentration camp).

Still Full of Hate

There were some places where Jews were still in danger, even after the Nazis were defeated. Many Jewish people were advised not to try to go home if they had lived in Poland. This was partly because their homes and families were gone but also because of the attitude of many Poles. Harry Balsam was a young Polish Jew who went to the station to make his way back to Poland:

> We met Jews getting off the train who had come back from Poland. They said we must be mad to try to go back, they had been lucky to get out alive. The Poles, they said, were still killing Jews.

Between 1945 and 1946 over 1,000 Jewish people were murdered in liberated Poland, by Polish people.

Rebuilding Europe

By the time the war ended, some parts of Europe had been at war for well over five years, and it showed. Cities, towns, roads, railway lines, and bridges had all been bombed. This destruction made moving around difficult, and almost everyone was trying to do just that. The **Allies** were still moving on to occupy all of Germany, trying to sort out areas they were responsible for. At the same time, they were trying to capture German soldiers and **Nazis** who had taken part in the **Holocaust.** German soldiers threw away their uniforms and tried to get back to Germany disguised as civilians. German civilians who had moved to **occupied** Europe also tried to get back to Germany. People from all of the Nazi **camps,** including prisoner-of-war camps, tried to make their way home, too.

Looting

Not only was it hard to travel, it was hard to find food, clothes—almost anything people needed to survive. Even soldiers from the Allied armies took things from the local people. Many people who had been prisoners in German camps took things from the local people, too. It was impossible for the Allies to act as a police force and control looting. Natalia Karpf, a survivor from Belsen, remembers:

> *Some women went into the flats* [apartments] *and took away suitcases of clothes, but I didn't. The women said: "But they're yours—they robbed you of all your things." But I didn't want to. What did I take? A small sack of sugar and a dress to replace my uniform.*

Sweeping Out the Garbage!

In 1940, the Germans had occupied Alsace (an area of Europe that had belonged to both France and Germany at various times). The Nazis produced a poster very similar to the one shown here. The 1940 poster showed "French rubbish [garbage]" being swept out. It suggested that the people of Alsace would be only too glad to get rid of all that "French trash" and accept the Nazis. The poster shown here was produced in 1945 in Alsace. It deliberately copies the 1940 poster but shows the sweeping out of "German trash," instead.

NORWAY
SWEDEN
DENMARK
North Sea
Baltic Sea
GREAT BRITAIN
NETHER-LANDS
IRELAND
EAST GERMANY
POLAND
USSR
BELGIUM
WEST GERMANY
CZECHOSLOVAKIA
FRANCE
AUSTRIA
SWITZERLAND
HUNGARY
ROMANIA
YUGOSLAVIA
ITALY
Adriatic Sea
BULGARIA
Black Sea
GEORGIA
SPAIN
PORTUGAL
Mediterranean Sea
ALBANIA
GREECE
TURKEY
N
W
E
S
0 km
500 km
0 miles
300 miles
Territory gained by USSR in 1945
Countries under communist control
Communist but independent
Iron Curtain

A New World

Once the war was over, Europe was divided up again. This time, the division was between countries that believed in **Communism** and those that did not.

Never Again

As the war ended, most countries were determined to stop another world war from breaking out. The same had been done after World War I (1914–1918). An organization called the League of Nations, with representatives from many different countries, had been set up to prevent another war. It had failed. Its failure was mainly because some important countries, like the United States and Germany, were not in the League. Also, the League had no real power to stop fighting when it broke out. So in 1941, while World War II was still going on, the United States and Britain signed an agreement called the Atlantic Charter. It was a list of ideas that they believed would prevent another war, including agreeing that war was wrong and that the treaty that ended the war should be fair. By January 1942, another 26 countries had signed the charter. They called themselves the United Nations (UN).

The UN

The United Nations set up organizations that began working to deal with the chaos the war was already creating. It decided that part of its work should be helping people and countries in distress. The organizations included the United Nations Relief & Rehabilitation Administration (UNRRA), set up in 1943 to provide food, medicine, clothes, and other kinds of help to countries **liberated** from the Nazis. After the war, the UN drew up a new set of rules that included respecting treaties and working for peace, and encouraged as many countries as possible to join. It set up medical and financial help for developing countries as well as countries damaged by war. The UN encouraged countries to see themselves as part of a worldwide family, not as separate, competing countries. The UN had the power to set up its own army to keep peace in member countries. It did not have a permanent army. Instead, it was to set up an army only when it was needed, using soldiers from all UN countries.

What About Germany?

The **Allies** had a problem over what to do about Germany. One of the causes of the war that had just ended had been the Treaty of Versailles. This treaty, which had ended World War I, had been very hard on Germany. It had taken away a lot of land and cut down Germany's army, air force, and navy. It had also insisted that Germany pay to repair war damage in other European countries. The Germans had resented the treaty and the government that accepted it. The **Nazis** had used this resentment to get into power, promising to put the treaty right. If that treaty had been too hard, what should the treaty that ended World War II be like? There were a lot of people who were determined that Germany should pay for starting both world wars, and for the **Holocaust.**

Complete Surrender

The Allied armies were quite clear about what they wanted from Germany—total surrender. In 1944, they agreed that the peace had to include: "the complete disarmament and demilitarization of Germany." This meant that Germany should not be allowed to set up armed forces or make weapons.

On May 7, what was left of the German government surrendered entirely. By June 5, the Allies had taken over the government of Germany, saying: "In Germany there is no central government capable of running the country or carrying out the orders of the victorious powers."

So, an Allied council was set up to run Germany. It divided Germany into four sectors, run by the United States, Britain, France, and the Soviet Union. Germany's capital city, Berlin, was divided into four zones, too.

The New Germany

This map shows how Germany was divided up among the Allies immediately after the war.

Running Germany

The Allied countries ran each zone in their own way, although they each had a representative on the Allied Council, which was supposed to make sure things such as the railways and roads worked between the zones. The zones were like separate countries; people needed permission and **papers** to cross from one zone to the other. Because Berlin was inside the Russian zone, the British, French, and Americans had to pass through the Russian zone to get to their areas of Berlin. All of the Allies were allowed to take whatever food and equipment they needed from the Germans.

The Homeless

Europe had millions of homeless **refugees** after the war. Added to the many Holocaust survivors were Germans who had lost their homes in bombing or the fighting that followed. Many German families who had settled in Poland and other places as the German empire expanded left these places to return to Germany, fearing that they would be badly treated if they stayed.

Refugees

Bombed-out refugees had to cope as best they could. Julia Kraut, bombed out of Hildesheim, had found a temporary home for herself and her children in a barn on a farm. The family lived there for five years, but life was hard:

> *Once when I asked for milk for the baby, the farmer said it had all been taken by the soldiers. The skimmed milk, I was told, was needed for the pigs. The children could play in the orchard, but could not eat the apples that fell from the trees. We had to go and dig for potatoes in the fields when the farmer had cleared them. The rule was always the same: first the Allies, then the farmer and his animals, then us.*

On the Move

The upheaval at the end of the war led to situations like the one in this photo. It shows a road, luckily with no bomb damage at this point, being used by a mix of people. There are advancing army tanks. There are **refugees** leaving their homes trying to get away from trouble. There are refugees trying to get back home. There are people trying to move from the zone controlled by one set of Allies to another zone. Finally, there are newly released prisoners-of-war trying to get back home.

The Allies Fall Out

At first, dividing up Germany seemed to work. The **Allies** began to break up the German army, to dismantle the factories that had been working for the war effort, to set up new, peaceful industries. There was one big problem. While they were fighting Hitler, the Allies had been able to forget their political differences. Once the war was over, though, these differences sprang up again. The Soviet Union was a **communist** country. The western countries were against communism and were worried it might spread to the West.

There was disagreement over the newly freed countries in Eastern Europe, such as Poland and Czechoslovakia. Britain, the United States, and France wanted these countries to elect their own governments. The Soviet Union, which still had troops in these countries, wanted them to have communist governments tied to the communist Soviet Union. In January 1947, the U.S. and Britain joined their zones together. This made the Soviet Union nervous. In June 1947, the U.S. started pouring money into Europe under a scheme called the Marshall Plan. The U.S. said it was providing money because it was in everyone's interest to get Europe back to normal as soon as possible. The Soviet Union, opposed to the political system of the United States, did not want this aid. The Soviet government feared that the U.S. was "buying" countries like Poland away from communism (which is partly what the U.S. was trying to do). The Soviet government set up its own organization, called Cominform, and forced these countries to join that, instead. By the end of 1948, the Soviet **Red Army** had made sure that Communists won the elections in Czechoslovakia, Poland, Hungary, Bulgaria, and Romania.

The Iron Curtain

In June 1948, the Soviet government closed off their zone. People could not go in or out, or use the roads, railways, or canals that crossed the zone. A line had been drawn between East and West, and Berlin was on the Russian side of that line, along with all of the new communist countries. Winston Churchill, the war-time British Prime Minister, made a famous speech in which he said: "An **Iron Curtain** has descended across the continent of Europe."

It looked as if another war might break out over who controlled Berlin. In the end, the Allies did not attack. They simply flew supplies into their zones in Berlin. The Soviet Union gave in and agreed to divide Berlin in two. The crossing point was to be guarded, and people could only cross at set checkpoints if they had the right **papers.**

Taking Sides

Then, the two sides began to set up agreements with other countries—very much like alliances made in case of war. In April 1949, the East–West divide hardened when the western powers set up the North Atlantic Treaty Organization (NATO), which most of the western powers joined over the next ten years. In 1955, the communist countries set up a similar set of alliances—the Warsaw Pact. This division affected politics all around the world over the next 50 years. Despite the devastation of the war, despite the horrors of the **Holocaust,** the world seemed to be poised for war once again.

Berlin Divided

Once Europe was divided, the easiest place to cross between East and West was Berlin. As the East–West divide hardened, the communist government became more and more unhappy with the fact that East Germans could cross into West Germany. On August 13, 1961, the East Germans built a high, guarded wall between the two halves of the city—the Berlin Wall. The rest of West Berlin was surrounded by a "Country" Wall, to prevent travel between West Berlin and the surrounding countryside.

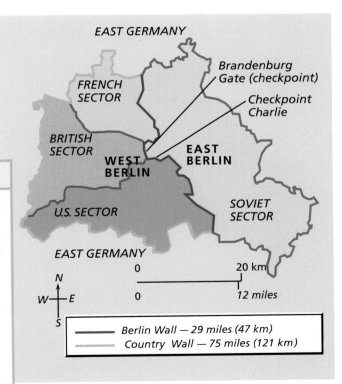

EAST GERMANY

FRENCH SECTOR

Brandenburg Gate (checkpoint)

Checkpoint Charlie

BRITISH SECTOR

WEST BERLIN

EAST BERLIN

U.S. SECTOR

SOVIET SECTOR

EAST GERMANY

N
W — E
S

0   20 km

0   12 miles

——— Berlin Wall — 29 miles (47 km)
——— Country Wall — 75 miles (121 km)

Rebuilding Lives

Clearly, the war and the **Holocaust** ripped places and lives apart. Most survivors were desperate to find out what had happened to their families and to rebuild their lives. The chaos at the end of the war made this hugely difficult, though. The United Nations Relief & Rehabilitation Administration (UNRRA) tried to cope with the chaos. The United States also sent medicine and food to Europe. Many survivors went to **Displaced Persons (DP) camps** run by various organizations from various countries. These camps were set up to help all those who were left homeless and separated from their families by the war. The people who worked at the camps all tried to help DPs find their families and decide where to start their new lives. It was slow work because of the huge numbers of people who needed help. There were about 30 million displaced people in Europe when the war ended. By 1947, there were still 850,000 without homes. Of these, 175,000 were **Jewish.**

Getting Healthy

One of the first steps in rebuilding lives was to get people healthy again. Most people who had been in the **camps** were ill; many were starving. Dr. Hadassah Rosensaft, a young Jewish doctor working in Belsen camp, in Germany, remembers one difficulty in the early days of the DP camps. It was hard to get enough **Allied** doctors and nurses, so German doctors and nurses were brought in:

> The psychological effects were bad enough on me—imagine what it was like for the severely ill. I said to Colonel Johnston [who was in charge of the hospital]: "Johnny, I can't take these people." But they were all there was. It took me a week to bring myself to work with them; I had to, for the sake of my patients.

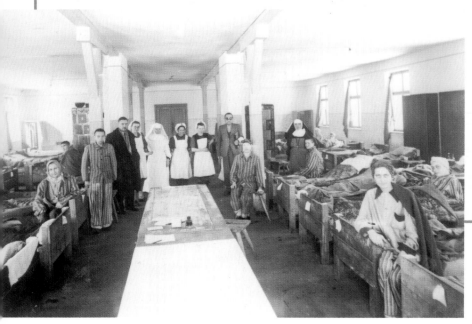

Helping the Children

The children in this photograph are being given new clothes by UNRRA workers. Gitta Sereny, a young UNRRA worker, spent a year and a half working with children in DP camps and special children's centers. The children had had many different experiences. Some had been in camps, others had lived in hiding or had been taken from their families and been brought up by Germans. Gitta found that dealing with their misery day after day without being able to make the problems go away affected her deeply:

> I sank deeper and deeper into the misery that the Nazis had caused. The sorting out of all the "unaccompanied" children was one of the most difficult tasks of the UNRRA.

Finding Families

Zvi Dagan, a young Jewish boy **liberated** at Terezín, in Czechoslovakia, remembers:

> The first thing people did was to gather information about surviving families. They asked relatives, the Red Cross, inmates from other camps, anyone at all. Mostly, the news was bad. I found out that my father was killed on a death march two weeks before liberation. I later discovered my brother was killed in Skarzysko-Kamienna **labor camp** (in Poland). He caught dysentery and the camp commandant shot him.

Moving On

Dr. Rosensaft remembers:

> We all wanted to leave the DP camps, but if we wanted to emigrate outside of Germany or Eastern Europe we had to stay and apply and do the paperwork.

Because there were so many people who wanted to leave Eastern Europe, it was hard to find places for them to go all at once. The Allies had assumed that people would want to go back to the places they had lived in before the war. This was not the case for a large number of people, especially people from Eastern Europe. Their homes were gone—in some cases whole villages and towns had been destroyed. Many people also feared, rightly, that they would not be welcome, especially those Jewish people who had lived in Poland before the war.

Otto Frank

Many people from western Europe who survived the **Holocaust** went home once the war ended. Otto Frank had left Germany with his wife, Edith, and two daughters, Anne and Margot, when the **Nazis** came to power. They went to Amsterdam. When the Nazis **occupied** the Netherlands, the Franks went into hiding, but they were eventually caught and sent to Auschwitz **camp.** After the war, Otto learned that his family members were dead. He returned to Amsterdam. He was lucky. His employees had kept his business going and gave it back. Other people returned home to find that their homes and businesses had been taken over by people who refused to give them back.

Eastern Europe

Jews who wanted to return to their homes in Eastern Europe faced many problems. Natalia Karpf, a young Jewish woman **liberated** from Auschwitz, went to the station, hoping to get to Krakow in Poland, to find out about her family:

> *On the way we met some Jews. They said: "You're crazy! Back to Krakow? There are too many **anti-Semites** there. Go someplace else." But we wanted to find our people, so we went.*

Natalia was lucky. The Polish people in the apartment her husband's parents had owned gave it back. People were not always kind, but she was not treated badly. However, those who returned to Poland were trapped when it became **communist.** The government banned emigration and did not allow it until 1957.

The United States and Canada

Many people ended up in the United States and Canada, even if they did not go there right after the war. Both countries had **quotas,** before and after the war, to keep huge numbers of people from flooding in at once. However, to many people in Europe after the war, the U.S. and Canada seemed like rich, almost magical places where the horrors of war could be forgotten. So, they applied to live there. While they waited to be accepted, they lived somewhere else, anywhere that would take them.

Going to Palestine

The question of going to Palestine was an especially difficult one. Even before the war, many Jewish people saw Palestine as the historical home of the Jews and wanted to live there. Unsurprisingly, the Arab Palestinians living there did not want large numbers of Jewish people moving to their country and taking it over, so they resisted. The British, who were in control of Palestine at the time, tried to restrict Jewish emigration to Palestine, before and after the war, to keep the Arabs happy. Some people in DP camps after the war decided: "So the British won't let you go legally. Defy them. Go illegally. If you want to go to Palestine, you should." Many people tried to get into Palestine without permission.

Moving Around

Many people moved around before settling down. The Hoffman family is one example. They had lived in Kraków before the war and lived in hiding there and in the surrounding countryside all through the war. After the war they lived in Kraków at first, but tried to get **exit visas** before the government stopped people from leaving Poland. They were not successful. They were trapped in Kraków for thirteen years and had two daughters, Eva and Alina. The family was never physically harmed. However, they had to deal with a lot of prejudice against Jews. For example, Eva's mother was once asked by a Christian friend (a well-educated doctor's wife) if Jews really mixed Christian blood in their Passover bread.

As soon as the emigration ban was lifted in Poland, in 1957, their friends began to leave and the Hoffmans applied to leave, too. At once, Mr. Hoffman had his job taken away for daring to apply to leave. The family lived in hardship for the two years it took to get all the paperwork sorted out. They emigrated to Vancouver, Canada, in 1959, where a friend had offered to give them a home and feed them until they could find work.

Lost Children

One of the most difficult problems for the UNRRA was the question of what to do with the children that the **Nazis** had decided to "Germanize." During the war, as they swept through Eastern Europe, the Nazis took tens of thousands of children from parents the Nazis saw as "subhuman." They gave these children to "good German" families to raise as German children. Some children were just babies when they were taken. Many had been with their new families for years and had forgotten their real parents. When the war ended, though, these parents went to the UNRRA and other organizations looking for their children. Some children settled well when they returned to their birth parents. Others found it much harder.

Finding the Children

Gitta Sereny, who worked for UNRRA after the war, spent some time trying to reunite "Germanized" children with their families. She remembers two children, Marie and Johann, who the UNRRA had been told might have been Germanized. The children were clearly much loved by the German family. The German family told Gitta that the Nazi officials who gave them the children had told them they were "German orphans." However, a Polish family claimed Marie and Johann—Marie had a small birthmark that was unmistakable. The children were taken from the German family and sent to a children's center before being returned to their birth parents. Gitta visited the center:

> The children's appearance, Johann's very hostile reaction to me and Marie's awful stillness, shook me deeply. Marie was crumpled in a chair, eyes closed, sucking her thumb. She was refusing to speak, wet the bed, and would only take food from a bottle. Johann raced up as soon as he saw me, shouting "You! You!" and hit and kicked me. It made you ask what was the best thing for these children.

Looking for a Family

This little girl is one of hundreds photographed by the UNRRA in the hope that someone from her family would see the photo, recognize her, and reclaim her.

This photo shows four of "the Boys" arriving in England in 1945.

The Boys

In June 1945, the British government offered to take 1,000 **Jewish** orphans under the age of sixteen from the **camps.** They could stay in Britain for two years, after which planning a future for them would be easier. At first, the UNRRA said there were no children alive, but eventually 732 were found and flown to England. They were called "the Boys" because most of them were boys. Girls had been much less likely to survive the camp system because the Nazis had been more likely to see boys as useful and keep them as workers rather than kill them.

Journey to England

Sala Newton-Kaye, one of the Boys, remembers flying to England, with 300 other boys in twelve bomber planes. "So many were sick from the flying. We sat on the floor of the plane with blankets, being ill. But what excitement! What joy!"

Henry Golde, another Boy, was pleased, but scared, too:

> Was I doing the right thing going to England? A strange new country, a language I didn't know. Should I have gone back to Poland? No, there was nothing left but bad memories. There were three hundred of us, I was not alone. They were my family.

The Lake District

Most of the Boys were taken to a special hostel at Crosby-on-Eden, in the Lake District of Britain. Abraham Zwirek, a young Polish boy, remembers: "When I woke in the morning I thought I was in Heaven. There were white sheets on the bed and white bread to eat." Pinkus Kurnedz, also from Poland, remembers the food: "White bread, milk, and cakes twice a day. I can still remember going to the cinema for the first time. The local people were very kind."

The Boys had some trouble adjusting to their new life at first. But eventually they settled in. By 1947, they had moved to hostels in various places to look for work. Many of the Boys decided to stay in England. Others left, going to Israel, the U.S. and Canada. They still keep in touch. They are each other's family.

Palestine or Zion?

Zion was the ancient **Jewish** name for Jerusalem. Thousands of years earlier, in Biblical times, Jerusalem and the lands around it (called Palestine) had been the homeland of the Jews. Some Jews believed that this land still belonged to them, and that Jews should go back there to live. These people called themselves Zionists.

In 1914, Palestine was controlled by Turkey. When World War I broke out in 1914, the British wanted the Arab people living in the Turkish empire to fight with the British against the Turks. The British promised that if the Arabs helped them, the British would make sure they governed their own countries. But, in 1917, the British also promised Jews a "national home" in Palestine. At the end of the war, the Turks were driven out of Palestine. How could the British keep both of their promises?

Palestine

The British decided to allow Palestine to become an Arab state, but to allow Jews to live there, too. In order to keep Palestine from being overrun by Jews, however, they had to restrict the numbers of Jewish people who could move there—even when they were trying to flee **Nazi** Germany in the 1930s. After World War II, Zionists toured the **DP camps** pressing Jewish people to go to Palestine, even though the British had set a **quota.** Many of them did go, trying to get into Palestine by land and sea. The United States urged the British to let them in. The Arabs pressed the British to keep them out. The British tried to turn most of the **refugees** back, sometimes by force. But, by 1947, the British felt that they could no longer keep control in Palestine, and they handed the problem over to the UN.

National Feeling

Many Jewish people who survived the war felt the need for a Jewish homeland. Zionists designed a flag for the state of Israel that they were urging the **Allies** to set up in Palestine. These people in a DP camp are waving that flag.

Israel

The UN decided to split Palestine into two states—one for the Arabs and one for the Jews. However, the Palestinian Arabs did not agree to this plan because much of the best land was to be given to the Jewish state, even though it was owned and occupied by Arabs. The Palestinians felt they had been promised control of their country by the British and did not see why their country should be carved up and given away to other people.

In May 1948, the Jews in Palestine announced that they were setting up their own state, to be called Israel, in the land that had been allocated to them by the UN. The new state immediately came under attack from the armies of the neighboring Arab states, who supported the Palestinians. During the fighting, hundreds of thousands of Palestinians were forced to flee their homes. By the end of the war, the Israelis controlled far more of Palestine than the UN originally said they should have. The Palestinians who had been forced out of this area were not allowed to return and became refugees in the surrounding countries.

Coming home

Over the next few years, over a million Jews flooded into Israel. They set up industries, cities, and farms. The Israeli government was determined not to turn people away, not to behave the way that other governments had behaved toward Jews looking for shelter before and after the war. Eva Hoffman's mother, considering leaving Poland in 1957, wrote to David Ben-Gurion, the first Prime Minister of Israel. She asked if, were the family to move to Israel, Eva would still be able to continue with her piano playing. A handwritten letter came back from Ben-Gurion, saying: "Be assured, we do not like to let talent go to waste in Israel. There are excellent music teachers here—if necessary we will pay her fees. We'll take care of her."

A Kibbutz

A kibbutz was a farm in Israel that everyone worked on and everyone was supported by. The children in the photograph are harvesting olives on a kibbutz. Everyone was encouraged to work hard on a kibbutz, no matter how young.

Long-term Effects

The **Holocaust** not only destroyed people's lives while it was happening. Those who survived the Holocaust were deeply affected by it forever because of their experiences. Survivors often remained fearful and uncertain. Many never felt settled in a community again. People who went to live in another country had to cope with language problems, as well as all of the other problems of fitting in.

Different Lives

Many survivors of the Holocaust remember that before the war their parents had high expectations for them. They were being educated to become professional people—doctors, lawyers, and teachers. The war had stopped their education and, once the war was over, they found that they were expected to become self-supporting as soon as possible. Unless they were found and taken in by family members who had escaped the Holocaust, there was no one willing to pay for further education for them. They had to take whatever work they could. Esther Brunstein had lived through the war as a young girl in the Lodz **ghetto** and Auschwitz, both in Poland. She came to Britain after the war and remembers:

> I went to Sweden directly after the war. Then a **Jewish** family in Romford, England, said they would take me in to do the housework and so on. That meant I could be in England, where my brother, Perec, was. So I went. I longed to continue my education, to become a nurse. But no one was prepared to give me my keep while I tried to replace my lost years.

Learning a Trade

Perec Zylberberg, Esther Brunstein's brother, remembers:

> We weren't encouraged to take up further studies. The Committee that was caring for us didn't have much money and was not expected to keep going for long. With very few exceptions, everyone was directed to some sort of occupation so they could make a living.

Perec, shown here on the right in the Lodz ghetto, had been an apprentice weaver. In England, after the war, he trained as an electrician and then as a tailor. In 1958, he emigrated to Canada, where he still lives.

Affected Families

Many Holocaust survivors married and had families. They worked hard at building new lives. Many of them married other survivors or people they met in the years after the war—liberators or people who helped them to find new homes. Their children, and others, were affected by the fact of the Holocaust. Some children lived very sheltered lives, their parents full of anxiety. Anna Karpf, whose parents both survived the Holocaust, remembers:

> My family was big on coats. All through my adolescence and beyond we'd have huge arguments about them. My parents never thought I wrapped up warm enough. It wasn't until later that I realized that, for my parents, cold wasn't just the weather. It was the dangerousness of anything outside the home. All parents probably worry, but our parents' fears were based not on what might happen, but on what had happened. They'd lost so much that they were naturally frightened about losing more.

Kristallnacht, November 9 and 10, 1938

Many survivors remember not just the camps of the Holocaust, but also the way many ordinary people joined in **Nazi**-organized violence against Jewish people.

Moving Around

This poem, by the Polish survivor Jerzy Ficowski, sums up how many survivors and their children felt guilty about those who did not survive, even though they could not have saved them.

> I did not manage to save
> a single life
>
> I did not know how to stop
> a single bullet
>
> and I wander round cemeteries
> which are not there
> I look for words
> which are not there
> I run
>
> To help where no one called
> To rescue after the event
>
> I want to be on time
> Even if I am too late.

Looking for Justice

The **Allies** all over **Nazi-occupied** Europe were shocked by what they found when they **liberated** the **camps.** Many felt that the Nazis involved in the **Holocaust** had to be punished. What they had done to people they saw as **undesirables,** especially **Jewish** people, could not just be accepted as something that happened during a war—it was a "war crime." The Allies wanted those who had helped in the Holocaust to be tried for these crimes. Legal punishment of the Nazis began after liberation. All through the countries that the German army had occupied, people who had helped the Nazis were tried and executed. First, though, the Allies had to catch the war criminals.

Friend or Foe?
In the confusion of the early days of liberation, it was hard for the Allies to know who to arrest. Nazis, especially camp guards and **SS** officers, threw away their uniforms and tried to escape.

Many of them succeeded. Very few people admitted to being a Nazi, or even a Nazi supporter, unless there was clear evidence that they were. Innocent people found themselves in danger, too. Leon Greenman, an English Jew liberated from Buchenwald, was told that he could take a jacket belonging to an SS officer. He did, and got someone to change the buttons, which had SS markings. Of course, the SS did the same thing to their jackets. While waiting for a plane to England he was nearly shot by a sentry who then arrested him:

After a while the door opened and four or five British prisoners-of-war came in. They had been called in to find out if I was who I said I was. I had to answer all sorts of questions about London and so on. I felt insulted, because they clearly thought I might have been a spy or an ex-Nazi.

He was eventually released.

Nazi or Not?

The Allies had to sift out the Nazis in the army and among ordinary people. It was not easy in either case. German soldiers were rounded up and put into prisoner-of-war camps, like this one in France, until they could all be questioned to find out their part in the war.

A Safe Place?

Buenos Aires, the capital of Argentina in South America, became a hiding place for thousands of Nazis on the run.

Running Away

Secret Nazi networks, called **ratlines,** smuggled thousands of Nazis to South America. They provided false **papers,** homes, money, jobs, even plastic surgery for those who feared their faces were too well-known. Some South American governments agreed with many Nazi ideas. They were glad to have the technical skills of Nazi scientists and engineers. They refused to put Nazis on trial or help other governments to prosecute them. They refused to hand them over, even when they were given evidence of their crimes. For example, General Perón of Argentina provided over a thousand blank passports for escaping Nazis. Hundreds of millions of Reich marks, the money of Nazi Germany, were transferred to banks in Buenos Aires, the capital of Argentina, in the last years of the war and after the war. One of the biggest Argentinian shipping firms, run by Alberto Dodero, smuggled thousands of boatloads of Nazis from Italy to Argentina.

More Surprising Helpers

Other countries helped Nazis escape, too. These countries helped secretly and hoped their help would never be discovered. They included Switzerland and the Vatican (the part of Rome run by the Pope, as head of the Catholic Church). Both were supposed to be neutral in the war—that is, they did not take sides. Sometimes they simply did not stop others from helping Nazis. For example, Argentinians in Switzerland moved money for the Nazis from Swiss banks to Argentina. They also ran ratlines through Switzerland. The Swiss government ignored it.

Switzerland and the Vatican were also more actively involved in helping Nazis to escape. There is evidence that the Swiss police smuggled Nazis out of the country. Meanwhile, in 1947, the U.S. State Department described the Vatican as "the largest single organization involved in the illegal movement of immigrants"— smuggling Nazis. Some high-ranking Catholic officials in the Vatican not only allowed ratlines to pass through, but were also accused of helping to provide false documents.

Catching Nazis

Many **Nazis** escaped in the chaotic conditions after the war, especially those who could afford to pay **ratlines** to help them. Many more remained in Germany. The **Allies** had two separate problems to face in Germany. They had to get the government working again, hopefully without Nazis in charge, and they had to catch as many Nazis as they could and bring them to trial.

"Denazification"

The Allies agreed that the German government that was set up after the war ought not to contain people who had been active members of the Nazi Party. They agreed that people should be interviewed in a process of denazification—arresting all "top" Nazis and making sure that all Nazi supporters were removed from jobs in government or in important businesses. Frank Foley had worked in the British embassies in Germany before the war. He returned to Germany to run the British denazification system in the British zone in Berlin. He had a difficult job. The Nazis had insisted that everyone who worked in the government and in business in Nazi Germany had to join the Nazi Party. So, everyone had been a member of the Nazi Party whether they believed in Nazi ideas or not. The Allies needed German civilians to help them get things going again. James Gibson, a British official in Berlin working on the denazification, remembers: "If a person was efficient and seemed O.K. and said they'd only joined the Nazis because they had to, then you tended to believe them and let them get on with it."

Breaking Up Ratlines

Frank Foley also tried to track down and break up ratlines. Foley was interested in breaking up the organization *Deutsche Revolution*, because he heard it had the most efficient escape routes out of Europe. One of Foley's people tricked Kurt Ellersiek, a leader of *Deutsche Revolution*, into giving them information to be able to carry out a raid on February 23, 1947, and arrest over 120 Nazis.

Catching Nazis

Outside Germany the Allies did not carry out a policy of denazification. They just tried to catch Nazis. Here, an informant in Oslo is helping the British Army to identify **SS** men.

A Different View of Justice

After the war, some **Jewish** people were angry at how slowly the Allies were arresting Nazis and bringing them to trial. They were concerned that as time passed more and more Nazis were escaping. The Israeli government chased Nazis by legal means, but there were some Jews, especially young Jews who had survived the **ghettos** and the **camps,** who decided that all governments were moving too slowly.

The Avengers

In 1945, Abba Kovner, who had fought with resistance groups throughout the war, called on other survivors to form a group he called the Avengers. He said they should work to bring Nazis to justice more quickly than governments could. He quoted from the Psalms in the Bible, saying he wanted to "repay them for their iniquity and wipe them out for their wickedness." The Avengers used the chaos in Europe to cover their movement as they looked for chances to poison Nazis. They had decided that poison would be quick and one of the safest methods for the poisoners, who could be well away before the poison was taken. One of the Avengers found work in a bakery near Stalag 13, a prison camp for Nazis. He poisoned a big batch of bread for the camp.

No one knows how many died. News stories claimed thousands died, while the American army (in charge of guarding the camp) said people had gotten sick, but none had died. The Avengers felt they had been successful and planned to go on to use the same system in other places. However, Abba saw that war was brewing between Israel and the Arabs. He recalled the Avengers to fight for Israel in 1948. Later, they argued about what to do next. Some of the Avengers did not want to stop killing Nazis until 6 million were dead, the estimate at the time of the number of Jews killed in the **Holocaust.** Abba convinced them that it was more important to keep their new homeland of Israel safe than to have revenge. They did not return to Europe.

On Trial at Nuremberg

At first, the **Allies** did not completely agree about what should happen to the **Nazis** who were caught. The Americans and the Russians wanted a large public trial of as many leading Nazis as they could catch. The British were concerned that such a trial could lead to problems. How could anyone be let off? How could the trials be fair? In the end the British agreed to the trial. While the Allies had very few of the Nazi high command to put on trial, they had caught Hermann Goering, the most important person in the Nazi government after Hitler himself. They had also caught many less important Nazis who had clearly been involved in the **Holocaust.**

Interpreters

Because people from so many different countries were at the Nuremberg trials, a huge number of interpreters were needed so that everyone involved understood what other people were saying. This photo shows the interpreters section of the court at Nuremburg.

An Important Decision

In August 1945, the United States, Britain, and the Soviet Union had agreed to try the Nazi leaders for their actions during the war. The UN supported this decision. It was an important decision because it was the first time that so many different countries had agreed that crimes committed in wartime were so bad that they could not be excused by being at war.

The First Trial

There were many trials of Nazis, spread over many years. For the first series of trials, at Nuremberg, the Allies chose 22 defendants, from different parts of the Nazi government. The trials took a long time. The judges wanted to be seen as fair so they gathered as much evidence as they could. The first series of Nuremberg trials began in October 1945 and ended in October 1946. There was so much evidence given at the trials that it filled 42 large books by the time it had all been recorded.

Top Nazis on Trial?

What the Allies had hoped for was to put Adolf Hitler and other important Nazis on trial. They managed to catch very few of these people. Hitler killed himself when soldiers from the Soviet Union attacked Berlin. Heinrich Himmler, in charge of the SS and later the whole German army, was captured a few days after Germany surrendered, but he managed to take poison he carried with him, rather than go to trial. Joseph Goebbels, who organized Nazi **propaganda,** also killed himself and his wife and six children. Other Nazis who led the Holocaust, such as Martin Bormann and Adolf Eichmann (see pages 40–41), escaped to South America. The only important Nazi leader that the Allies could bring to trial was Hitler's former deputy and head of the German air force, Hermann Goering, shown in the picture. He was found guilty. Before he could be executed, he committed suicide.

The Charges
The 22 defendants on trial at Nuremberg were tried for four things:
- having "a common plan, or conspiracy"
- committing "crimes against the peace"
- committing "war crimes"
- committing "crimes against humanity"

The fourth accusation was tied most closely to the Holocaust, although the third one covered it, too.

The Verdicts
Of the 22 defendants at the first series of Nuremberg trials:
- 8 were found guilty of conspiracy.
- 12 were found guilty of crimes against peace.
- 16 were found guilty of war crimes.
- 16 were found guilty of crimes against humanity.

What Happened to Them?
- 3 were found not guilty of any of the listed crimes. They were released.
- 1 was imprisoned for 10 years.
- 1 was imprisoned for 15 years.
- 2 were imprisoned for 20 years.
- 3 were imprisoned for life.
- 11 were hanged.
- Goering was sentenced to be hanged, but killed himself.

Other War Criminals
Between 1945 and 1995, hundreds of thousands of people were arrested and tried for war crimes—there were nearly 90,000 in West Germany alone. Some were executed, and many more were imprisoned. Some were released, often because the courts felt that they had not been identified clearly. Tens of thousands of Nazis went unfound and unpunished—especially women, despite the fact that most female **camps,** or camps with female sections, had female **SS** guards.

The Hunt for Adolf Eichmann

While much of the world tried to forget the **Holocaust,** there were people committed to tracking down **Nazis.** One of these people was Simon Wiesenthal, a **camp** survivor who remembers clearly when he decided to devote his life to Nazi-hunting:

> *In 1944, an **SS** guard asked me how I would describe the camps, if I ever escaped. I told him I would tell the truth. The guard said no one would believe that anyone was capable of such brutality. I decided I had to make sure people had the facts, to root out Nazis and to make sure we never forget.*

Adolf Eichmann

This photograph shows Eichmann in 1940.

Wiesenthal has since caught, or helped to catch, over 1,000 Nazis. The most powerful of them was Adolf Eichmann. He had been in charge of the "Final Solution," the Nazis' attempt to murder all **Jewish** people in Nazi-**occupied** Europe.

On the Run

Adolf Eichmann tried to escape after the war but was captured by the American army and put into a prisoner-of-war camp. None of the **Allies** yet realized his involvement in the Holocaust. They treated him like an ordinary soldier. Eichmann knew they would eventually find out his involvement in the Holocaust. He escaped from the prison and altered his **papers.** When he was caught again, after a few weeks, he was calling himself Otto Eckmann. This time, the American troops that caught him sent him to a camp that was just 35 miles (56 kilometers) from Nuremberg, where the Allies were preparing to conduct a war trial.

Evidence of Eichmann's crimes began to pile up, and the Allies were actively looking for him. "Eckmann" realized that it was dangerous to stay where he was. The Allies were questioning everyone about the Nazi leaders. Eichmann could not be sure that none of the other prisoners would recognize him. If they did, they might give him away. He escaped again and headed for the mountains.

There, with the help of other Nazis, he received forged identity papers. Thus, he did not have to change his own papers, and he could use a totally different name. He became Otto Henninger, a chicken farmer. He hoped that the hunt for him would be called off when he could not be found. He hoped to live quietly as Henninger and wait until things calmed down.

Leaving Europe

Things did not calm down. In 1948 Eichmann fled to Italy and lived for some time in a monastery while a Nazi **ratline** got him new forged papers. He became Ricardo Klement. In 1950, the ratline helped him to escape to Argentina. He hid in a small mountain village until the ratline told him that they were sure none of the groups looking for him had any idea where he was. In 1952, Eichmann sent for his family and they went to live in Buenos Aires.

Eichmann worked in a local car factory, where he quickly rose from being an ordinary worker to being the foreman.

It was there that Mossad, the Israeli secret service, found him in 1959. Mossad knew the Argentinian government was sympathetic to the Nazis and would not hand Eichmann over for trial, nor would they bring him to trial themselves. So, Mossad snatched Eichmann in May 1960 and took him to a secret hiding place. They forced him to sign a statement saying that he was willing to go back to Israel for trial. Then they drugged him and flew him out of Argentina to Israel. The Argentinian government complained because Mossad was working for the Israeli government and the Argentinians said that governments should respect each other's laws. They did not force the Israelis to return Eichmann, however.

The Trial

Eichmann was tried in Israel. The trial began in April 1961 and was adjourned in August. He was found guilty, and in December 1961, he was sentenced to death. He was executed at midnight on May 31, 1962.

Finding Nazi Loot

Justice was not simply a matter of hunting down and punishing **Nazis.** People had lost their homes, all of their possessions, and money. Museums and art galleries in **occupied** Europe had been stripped of their treasures. What happened to these things?

Art Treasures

Hitler and the Nazis often stressed the importance of "culture," as long as it was their kind of culture. They went to concerts and plays and they collected art. However, much of the art they "collected" came from museums and art galleries in countries they took over. There was a Special Staff section of the **SS** set up to do this. The Nazis also stole many works of art from **Jewish** people who left Germany after the Nazis came to power or who were sent to the camps.

The Nazis claimed that they were taking works of art away from museums to keep them safe from enemy bombing or other dangers of war. Among themselves, they talked of bringing these art treasures "home to the **Reich,**" where the Nazis believed they belonged. The Nazis had art historians make up various complicated stories that were supposed to show that the artists were really German. Some of the stolen art went straight into the collections of powerful Nazis. The rest was hidden away in safe, secret locations.

Other Valuables

Jewelry and other valuable possessions taken from Jewish people were often sold right away, outside Germany, to make money for the Nazis. The profits were paid into the National Bank of Germany under the false name of Max Heiliger. (Heiliger sounds like *Heil Hitler*, so it was easy for the Nazis who made deposits to remember.) This account provided money to Nazis to help them escape after the war.

The Lady with the Ermine

This valuable painting, *The Lady with the Ermine*, by the famous artist Leonardo da Vinci, was just one of the art treasures that the Nazis looted when they occupied Poland. It is now in the Czartoryski Museum, in Krakow, Poland.

Gold

The Nazis stole art treasures, jewelry, and many other possessions from their victims. Gold was what they wanted most, though, and they took it from people all over Europe. Many people, especially in the war years, turned their savings into gold. Unlike savings in a bank, gold could be used in any country in the world. The Nazis even took all of the gold from the teeth of the people they killed in the **death camps.** There was a special organization, called the Melmer Group, just for collecting this gold, melting it, down and storing it.

Hiding Stolen Gold

During the war, the Nazis used Swiss banks to move and store about 75 percent of their gold, worth over $400 million today. The Swiss were neutral, so they were not supposed to take sides in the war. However, Swiss banks had a reputation for dealing with anyone and for being very good at keeping secrets. This made the Swiss banks ideal for the Nazis, especially because Switzerland was not part of the Nazi Reich. Thus, if there was a problem and the Nazis had to leave the Reich in a hurry, they would still be able to reach the Swiss banks. Sweden and Portugal,which was also supposed to be neutral, traded with the Nazis and allowed them to use their banks, too.

Nazi Gold

This photo shows Lt. Gordon Rohrbach, of the American 7th Army, examining Nazi loot found in a cave built into the Konigsee mountains in Germany. This loot was Hermann Goering's collection and included silver and gold objects, and paintings.

Nothing Too Small

The Nazis stole many valuables. Nothing was too small for their attention. This was true of individual Nazis and the organization as a whole. Ruth Cyrus, a young Jewish lawyer who lived in hiding in Poland when it was under Nazi rule, remembers: "The SS would come to question you at home. And while they were talking you would see one of them put a paperweight in his pocket, another a cigarette case."

In the camps, everything taken from the prisoners was sorted, stored, and saved. In Auschwitz, the SS even saved shoes, worn-out toothbrushes, and false limbs.

Surviving, Remembering

In the 1950s, there was a strong feeling that World War II, and therefore the **Holocaust,** should be forgotten. Many people accused the survivors who wanted to talk about it of wallowing in misery, refusing to get on with life. It was clear that despite the reports from the **camps** at the end of the war, very few people had any clear idea of what the survivors had gone through. One British official, talking about the education of some of the Boys, a group of Jewish survivors in Britain, said disbelievingly: "You mean to say they did not give the children books to read in the camps?"

For the survivors, it was clear that remembering was vital. Many of them remember dying people in the camps saying: "You must live, survive. You must write it down, record it, tell it. You must make sure that people know what happened."

People kept secret records at the time—writings, photos, and paintings. As time has passed, it has become easier for survivors to tell their stories because people have become more willing to listen. Museums and memorials have been set up all over the world and people have worked hard to collect the stories of survivors, both written down and on film. Some survivors visit schools regularly and tell their stories over and over, to new generations of children. They are determined that the Holocaust not be forgotten.

Memorials

Auschwitz-Birkenau is the only **death camp** that the **Nazis** failed to destroy before the **Allies** arrived. It, and the nearby Auschwitz I camp, have been preserved as a memorial and a museum. This photo shows the memorial at Auschwitz-Birkenau.

Museums

There are museums about the Holocaust all over the world. Some are on or near the sites of camps. Others are set up far from where the Holocaust took place. This photo shows the United States Holocaust Memorial Museum in Washington, D.C. It is one of the museums that aims at teaching young people about the Holocaust. It has routes through the exhibits especially for young people to follow.

What Holocaust?

Although there have been more people willing to listen to survivors, another group of people have been speaking out, too. These are the people who deny that the Holocaust ever happened. These "Holocaust deniers" deliberately twist the facts to suggest that, while a few **Jewish** people were killed, there were no death camps and there was no Holocaust. The Nazis, they say, were just running tough prisoner-of-war camps. They are helped in their argument by the fact that the Nazis mostly did not talk openly about the "Final Solution," even in official documents. For example, Nazis talked about the "**resettlement** of Jews in the East" instead of murder. Despite this, however, enough documentation has survived to make denying the Holocaust absurd.

New Nazis?

One of the things that survivors hope is that their testimony will prevent the rise of another party like the Nazis. In an interview on October 29, 2001, Simon Wiesenthal said that the focus of his work was changing from tracking down Nazis to keeping track of the rise of neo-Nazi groups and people who deny the Holocaust. Wiesenthal, who lives in Austria, says:

> *There are now small groups in Germany and Austria who say that not everything about Nazism was bad. And one day, when the situation is good for them, they could grow into a far bigger, more dangerous, group.*

The fear that at some time the Holocaust might be repeated is a nightmare that the survivors hope their testimonies can prevent. Since the Holocaust, many people have used the words "never again," hoping that this will be so.

Caught in the Aftermath

Once the **Nazis** were defeated, survivors could not just return to their old lives. Those who had been **camp** prisoners found, on their release, that Europe was in chaos after the war. The following is how one survivor coped with the aftermath of the war.

Kitty Hart-Moxon

Kitty Hart-Moxon was born in Bielsko, Poland, in 1926. She was just twelve when war broke out in 1939. Her family moved to the Polish city of Lublin, only to be swept into a **ghetto,** where **Jewish** people were shut away from the rest of the population. She remembers:

> *In Lublin, most local Jews were **deported** to make way for dazed newcomers from Holland, France and elsewhere. Even as they struggled to understand the ghetto, the language, the system, they were shipped out so that another batch could be moved in. There was no time to coordinate any mass rising against the Nazis.*

In Hiding

Kitty's family tried to escape from Lublin more than once. But, without **papers**, it was hard:

> *The lack of documents was a constant danger. Every traveller had to register in every place they stayed for more than two days and also had to have an exit permit. As Jews were forbidden to travel at all, they did not have these documents.*

They eventually managed to escape and settled in a small Jewish village, in Poland, Zabia Wola. Someone told the Nazis about the village, though. Luckily, someone also told the villagers about the Nazis. Everyone who was able to get away did so. Kitty's father bought papers saying they were Polish, but not Jewish. He decided it was safest to split up. He told Kitty and her mother to go to Germany disguised as Polish workers. He felt the Nazis would be less likely to look for Jews inside Germany, which they thought was **Judenfrei**—Jew free. The plan worked for several years, but in 1943, one of the girls with whom they were working in a factory betrayed them to the Nazis.

Happier times

This photo shows Kitty on vacation in 1933 with her parents, her brother Robert, and her grandmother. Robert left Lublin to join the **partisans.** Their grandmother stayed behind in the village of Zabia Wola, where they hid when they first escaped from Lublin.

DP Camps

Survivors in **DP camps,** like Kassel camp shown here, held memorial services for friends and family who were Holocaust victims.

Auschwitz-Birkenau

Kitty and her mother were sent to Auschwitz camp. Then in 1944, they made a death march from Auschwitz, trailing from camp to camp in the freezing snow. Kitty remembers: "By now, my priorities were fixed. I made sure my tin mug was safely fastened around my waist with string and kept close to my mother."

Sometimes they were moved around by train, in open wagons, or cattle trucks. Kitty and her mother survived when they were left to die locked up in cattle cars. They were taken to Salzwedel camp, in Germany, early in 1945. The camp was **liberated** by the American army on April 13, 1945:

*In the second week of April the **SS** stopped taking work parties to the sugar refinery. The guards tossed a last helping of rotting beets and Swedes into the center of the camp and disappeared. At first, none of us dared try to break into the SS store. What if they were hiding, waiting for us to make a move before beating us up? Then we saw the American soldiers. At first they seemed not to notice us, but when we began to scream and wave, a couple of tanks came in our direction. The gates were smashed open. The men flinched from the kisses of the ecstatic, filthy, stinking girls who tried to climb all over them.*

Immediately after Liberation

The Americans had no food with them to give the women in the camp. They opened the gates and told them to help themselves: "Five of us set off to raid the town. We hammered on the door of the first house we took a fancy to and then forced it open."

Kitty and her friends found the family hiding in the cellar—two little girls with their mother and grandparents. They did not harm the family, but smashed up the house: "The only things I took away were useful things such as jam, flour, bottled fruit, and a woolen blanket for my mother."

After a three-day rampage in the town, the American army put up notices banning more raids.

Helping the Liberators

Kitty and her mother spoke English, so they were useful to the liberators:

*A few days after **liberation** I was taken by the Americans around the surrounding districts to see if I could spot **SS** men and women hiding as ordinary people. We found quite a few. I asked if I could take a coat from one of the SS women and they let me have it. One SS man was brought back to camp and given the job of carrying the corpses from sick bay—people were still dying from disease.*

Kitty and her mother also worked as translators: "One of my first tasks was to translate for the Russian and American officers as they worked out which areas each country would control." They decided that Salzwedel was in the Soviet zone and did not want to be stranded there:

We begged the Americans to take us with them as they pulled out, and went with them to a camp at Brunswick, still in Germany, but outside the Soviet zone.

Working for the British

Brunswick ended up in the British zone, so Kitty and her mother worked as translators for the British. They were supposed to stay in Brunswick, which was a **Displaced Persons (DP) camp**. Camps were set up all over Europe to house survivors while they recovered, for most were very ill. While they were there, various charity organizations tried to trace their relatives. Kitty and her mother, who were both well, were allowed to move into a house near the DP camp. They translated official documents at the camp and also traveled around translating at interviews and trials all over the area. Working to track down the SS was one thing. It was harder to help the British to prosecute Poles who had escaped from the DP camp to raid German farms for food: "It was difficult for me not to show where my sympathies lay."

A friend suggested that they move to a DP camp run by Quakers at Broitzem, near Brunswick. While there, Kitty worked in the welfare office and in the registration office, trying to help people in the camp trace their families.

Leaving

Kitty and her mother leaving their first DP camp in 1946.

Kitty, Now

Kitty Hart-Moxon still gives talks and writes books to make sure the **Holocaust** is not forgotten.

Looking for Family

Kitty and her mother worked hard for the **Allies,** but they also tried to track down their own relatives:

> For three months I spent all my off-duty time hitch-hiking between French, American, and British zones, between DP camps and Red Cross offices, trying to trace our family. I wanted to go back to Bielsko, but Mother was upset by the idea of me going into the Russian sector.

It took a while to get any news at all. When it came, it was not good:

> My father had been living on a farm near Tarnow, in Poland. The peasant he had lived with had worked hard to trace us, but had sad news. Somehow the **Gestapo** had found out he was Jewish. He was taken out of the village and shot through the head, then his body was thrown over a cliff.

Kitty's brother, Robert, had joined a Polish unit of the Soviet **Red Army** and was killed defending Stalingrad from the German Army. Kitty's grandmother was caught by the **Nazis** at Zabia Wola. She was sent to Belzec **death camp.**

No Survivors?

Other information about relatives trickled in:

> It began to seem as if Mother and I were the only survivors of our large family. We heard that our home had been looted and broken up—there was nothing to go back to. At last we heard that cousin Max and his wife, Lucy, had managed to escape to Russia. They had spent the war in Siberia. Max had tried to trace the family but had failed to find anyone and had gone to Egypt, then France, and finally settled in America.

A New Home

Kitty and her mother went to join relatives who had fled from Austria to Birmingham, England, in 1939. Kitty found work as a housekeeper but found it hard to adapt. People in England did not understand her situation. Her uncle had told her not to talk about the past. When she did mention it to English people, they were disbelieving. She trained as an X-ray technician and married in 1949. Since the 1960s, she has written, spoken, and made television programs about her experiences during the war.

Timeline

1933

January 30	Adolf Hitler and the **Nazi** Party come to power in Germany
February 27	Fire breaks out at the Reichstag, the German Parliament. Hitler and his political party, the Nazis, blame **communists** for the fire.
February 28	Hitler persuades the German President, Hindenburg, to pass a decree "For the Protection of the People and the State" that allows for the creation of **concentration camps**. The Nazis pressed for the camps pointing to fears of a "communist threat" after the Reichstag fire.
March 5	New elections are held. The Nazis win easily with intimidation.
March 17	The **SS** (short for "*Schutzstaffel*"—security staff) is set up as Hitler's bodyguard
March 21	Dachau, the first Nazi concentration camp, is set up. Concentration camps and **labor camps** are set up steadily after this.
April 1	**Jewish** shops in Berlin are boycotted.
April 7	Jewish government employees, including civil servants, teachers, and professors, lose their jobs.
April 26	The **Gestapo** (Nazi secret police force) is set up.
May 10	Books written by Jews, "degenerates," liberals, and Nazi opponents are burned.
July 14	Political parties other than the Nazi Party are banned in Germany.

1934

April 20	Heinrich Himmler is put in charge of the Gestapo.
July 20	The SS is no longer under the control of the army. They swear loyalty to Hitler alone and run their own organization.
August 2	Hitler makes himself *Führer*, sole leader of Germany.

1935

September 15	The Nuremberg Laws are passed against German Jews.

1937

	Jewish businesses are "**Aryanized.**"
July 16	Buchenwald concentration camp is set up.

1938

March 13	Germany takes over Austria.
November 9	Synagogues are burned and Jewish shops and homes are looted in Nazi-led violence against Jewish people known as *Kristallnacht*.

1939

September 1	Germany invades Poland. Nazis begin to pass laws against Polish Jews, restricting the work they can do, as in Germany in 1933–1936.
September 3	Britain and France declare war on Germany.
September 28	Germany and the Soviet Union split Poland up between them.

1940

February 12	The first group of Jews are deported from Germany to ghettos in Poland.
April 9	Germany invades Denmark and Norway.
May 10	Germany invades Belgium, France, Luxembourg, and the Netherlands.

1941

April 6	Germany invades Yugoslavia and Greece.
June 22	Germany invades the Soviet Union; mass executions of Jews take place.
September	Mass gassings at Auschwitz begin with Soviet prisoners-of-war. They then focus on Jews and become more regular from January 1942.
October 16	Mass **deportation** of German Jews to Poland begins.
December 7	Japan bombs American fleet at Pearl Harbor.
December 11	Germany and Italy declare war on the United States.

1942

January 20	Nazis discuss the "Final Solution" to Jewish problem at the Wannsee Conference.

1943

June 11	Himmler orders all **ghettos** to be closed and the people in them sent to the camps.

1944

April 9	Two Jews escape from Auschwitz and send news of the camp out of **occupied** Europe to the **Allies.** News of the camp cannot now be ignored.
From June	Death marches take place from camps in the east, moving westward in front of advancing Soviet troops.
June 6	Allied troops land in Normandy, France.

1945

January 17	The final death march from Auschwitz-Birkenau takes place. All prisoners who can walk are marched west, toward Germany, away from the advancing Allied armies.
January 27	Soviet troops reach Auschwitz.
April 11	American troops reach Buchenwald.
April 15	British troops reach Belsen.
April 29	American troops reach Dachau. Russian troops reach the outskirts of Berlin.
April 30	Hitler commits suicide in Berlin.
May 1	Goebbels commits suicide.
May 5	American troops reach Mauthausen. German army in Netherlands, Denmark, and north Germany surrenders.
May 7	Germany surrenders to the Allies.
November 20	Nuremberg trials of Nazi war criminals begin.

1946

October	The first group of war criminals are executed.

1950

	Adolf Eichmann flees to Argentina, using the false name Ricardo Klement.

1960

May	Mossad, the Israeli secret service, finds Adolf Eichmann hiding out in Buenos Aires, Argentina, kidnaps him, and takes him to Israel.

1961

April	Eichmann's trial starts. When it ends he is condemned to death and is executed in May 1962.

Glossary

Ally country that fought against Nazi Germany in World War II

anti-Semitism prejudiced against Jewish people; someone who does not like Jews is *anti-Semitic*

Aryan word used by the Nazis to mean people with northern European ancestors, without any ancestors from what they called "inferior" races, such as Poles, Slavs, or Jews. Aryans were usually blonde, blue-eyed, and sturdy.

camp *See* concentration camp, labor camp, and death camp.

communist person who believes that a country should be governed by the people of that country for the good of everyone in it. They believe private property—such as owning a home or a business—is wrong. They believe that the state should own and run everything—giving the people everything they need.

concentration camp prison camp set up by the Nazis under a special law that meant that the prisoners were never tried and were never given a release date. The Nazis could put anyone in these camps, for any reason or none, for as long as they wanted.

death camp camp set up by the Nazis to murder as many people, most of them Jewish, as quickly and cheaply as possible. Most of the victims were gassed.

deportation being sent away from a place and not allowed to return

displaced persons (DP) camp camp set up after World War II for people who had been taken from their homes and countries and separated from their families. Workers in these camps tried to trace families and help people return home.

Einsatzgruppen special units of the German army set up by the Nazis. These units went into eastern Europe at the same time as the army. Their job was supposedly to round up and kill civilians who were a danger to the Reich. In fact, they were told to kill Jews.

exit visa government document allowing someone to leave a country

Führer leader; title Adolf Hitler gave to himself as ruler of Germany

Gestapo secret police set up by the Nazis in 1933

ghetto area of a town or city, walled or fenced off from the rest of the city, where Jewish people were forced to live

Hitler Youth Nazi organization for boys that trained them to be fit and obedient to the Nazis. Boys were trained to become good soldiers. Girls had to join a girls' movement that trained them to be good wives and mothers.

Holocaust huge destruction or sacrifice. When it appears with a capital "H," it refers to the deliberate attempt by the Nazi government in Germany to destroy all of the Jewish people in their power.

Iron Curtain used to describe the physical division between capitalist and communist countries after World War II, as well as the ban on trade and information between them

Jew (Jewish) someone who follows the Jewish faith. The Nazis also called people Jews if they had Jewish ancestors, even if they had changed their faith.

Judenfrei "Jew Free;" a place with no Jewish people living there

kapo prisoner who was put in charge of other prisoners when they were working

labor camp camp set up by the Nazis that was a prison that used the prisoners as cheap labor

liberated used in this book to mean a place, especially a concentration camp, being freed from the control of the SS. Camps were liberated by Allied soldiers.

Nazi member of the Nazi Party. Nazi is short for *Nationalsozialistische Deutsche Arbeiterpartei*, the National Socialist German Workers' Party.

occupied used in this book to mean a country that has been captured by Germany and is ruled by Nazis supported by the German army

papers used in this book to mean all of the different documents needed under Nazi rule: identity card, work permit, travel permit, Aryan certificate, and so on

partisan someone who fights an army that has invaded and taken over his or her country

propaganda information and ideas that are worded and presented so that people will accept and believe them, even if they are not true

quota set amount of something. It is used in this book to refer to countries fixing the number of people allowed to come and live in that country from another country.

race group of people with the same ancestors

ratline network set up to help Nazis to escape after the war

Red Army name of the army of the Soviet Union

refugee someone fleeing the place where they live, usually in fear of his or her life

Reich empire. *See* Third Reich.

resettlement taking people away from one place and making them settle somewhere else. Jewish people who were moved to the ghettos and then to the camps by the Nazis were promised they would be "resettled" in the east.

resistance name given to groups formed in countries taken over by the Nazis to secretly fight the Nazis and try to drive them out of the country

SS (short for *Schutzstaffel*) security staff. The SS began as Hitler's personal bodyguard. Later, they ran concentration camps and death camps. Everyone in the SS swore loyalty to Hitler, rather than Germany.

Third Reich "the third empire." The Nazis saw their rule as the third German empire, with Hitler as the emperor, or *Führer*.

transport used in this book to refer to a trainload of people being sent to the camps

undesirable word used by the Nazis to describe any person that they did not approve of because of political beliefs, race, religion, or behavior.

Further Reading

Frank, Anne. *Diary of a Young Girl.* Columbus, Ohio: Prentice Hall, 1993.

Shuter, Jane. *Auschwitz.* Chicago: Heinemann Library, 1999.

Tames, Richard. *Anne Frank.* Chicago: Heinemann Library, 1998.

Tames, Richard. *Adolf Hitler.* Chicago: Heinemann Library, 1998.

Whittock, Martyn. *Hitler & National Socialism.* Chicago: Heinemann Library, 1996.

Wiesel, Elie. *Night.* New York: Bantam Books, 1982.

Willoughby, Susan. *The Holocaust.* Chicago: Heinemann Library, 2000.

Sources

The author and publisher gratefully acknowledge the publications from which written sources in this book are drawn. In some cases, the wording or sentence structure has been simplified to make the material appropriate for a school readership.

Altbeker Cyrus, Ruth. *A Jump for Life.* London: Constable & Robinson Ltd., 1997. (p. 43)

Engelmann, Bernt. *In Hitler's Germany.* Westminster, Md.: Schoken Books, Incorporated, 1988. (p. 17)

Fénelon, Fania. *Playing for Time.* Syracuse, N.Y.: Syracuse University Press, 1997. (p. 12)

Frister, Roman. *The Cap: The Price of a Life.* Cambridge, UK: Grove Books, Limited, 1999. (p. 9)

Gilbert, Martin. *The Boys: The Story of 732 Young Concentration Camp Survivors.* New York: Henry Holt & Company, 1997. (pp. 12, 17, 25)

Gilbert, Martin. *Never Again: A History of the Holocaust.* New York: Universe Publishing, 2000. (p. 33)

Greenman, Leon. *An Englishman in Auschwitz.* Portland, Oreg.: Vallentine Mitchell Publishers, 2001. (p. 34)

Hahn, Edith. *The Nazi Officer's Wife.* Brookline Village, Mass.: Abacus Press, 1999. (p. 16)

Hart-Moxon, Kitty. *Return to Auschwitz.* New York: House of Stratus, Incorporated, 2000. (pp. 46–49)

Hoffman, Eva. *Lost in Translation: A Life in a New Language.* New York: Penguin Putnam, Incorporated, 1990. (pp. 27, 31)

Lane, Allen and Gitta Sereny. *The German Trauma.* New York: Penguin, 2001. (pp. 25, 28)

Lebert, Stephan. *My Father's Keeper.* New York: Little, Brown and Company, 2000. (p. 7)

Karpf, Anna. *The War After.* London: Minerva Press, 1997. (pp. 18, 26, 33)

Rees, Laurence. *The Nazis: A Warning from History.* New York: The New Press, 1997. (p. 14)

Riley, Joanne. *Belsen: The Liberation of a Concentration Camp.* London: Routledge, 1981. (pp. 10, 11, 24, 25)

Smith, Michael. *Foley: The Spy Who Saved 10,000 Jews.* London: Hodder and Stoughton, 1999. (p. 36)

Townsend, Colin & Eileen. *War Wives.* New York: Grafton Publications, Incorporated, 1989. (p. 21)

Places of Interest and Websites

Florida Holocaust Museum
55 Fifth Street South
St. Petersburg, FL 33701
Visitor information: (727) 820-0100
Website: *http://www.flholocaustmuseum.org*

Holocaust Memorial Center
6602 West Maple Road
West Bloomfield, MI 48322
Visitor information: (248) 661-0840
Website: *http://holocaustcenter.org*

Holocaust Museum Houston
5401 Caroline Street
Houston, TX 77004
Visitor information: (713) 942-8000
Website: *http://www.hmh.org*

Simon Wiesenthal Center: Museum of Tolerance
Simon Wiesenthal Plaza
9786 West Pico Blvd.
Los Angeles, CA 90035
Visitor information: (310) 553-8403
Website: *http://www.museumoftolerance.com*

United States Holocaust Memorial Museum
100 Raoul Wallenberg Place, SW
Washington, D.C. 20024
Visitor information: (202) 488-0400
Website: *http://www.ushmm.org*

Website warning
1. Almost all Holocaust websites have been designed for adult users. They may contain horrifying and upsetting information and pictures.
2. Some people wish to minimize the Holocaust, or even deny that it happened at all. Some of their websites pretend to be delivering unbiased facts and information. To be sure of getting accurate information, it is always best to use an officially recognized site such as the ones listed on this page.
3. If you plan to visit a Holocaust website, ask an adult to view the site with you.

Disclaimer
All the Internet addresses (URLs) given in this book were valid at the time of going to press. However, due to the dynamic nature of the Internet, some addresses may have changed, or sites may have ceased to exist since publication. While the author and publisher regret any inconvenience this may cause readers, no responsibility for any such changes can be accepted by either the author or the publisher.

Index